Bound b

Spiritual & Practical Preparation for Entering the Marriage Covenant

Pastor Scott A. Burr

Strategic Book Publishing
New York, New York

Strategic Book Publishing
An imprint of AEG Publishing Group
845 Third Avenue, 6th Floor — #6016
New York, NY 10022
www.StrategicBookPublishing.com

ISBN: 978-1-60693-207-0
SKU: 1-60693-207-1

Printed in the United States of America

Contents

Preface

What holds marriages together? Is it love? Is it common interests? Or is there a deeper spiritual bond that binds couples together when they enter into holy matrimony. We believe the key to health and longevity in a marriage is rooted in understanding and recognizing the importance of "covenant." The purpose of this workbook is to provide ministers, marriage counselors and couples with a scripture-based foundation for entering that precious covenant. This workbook is not approached from a relational standpoint, but rather is embedded with covenant principles. It is our hope that ministers and marriage counselors will utilize this resource to once again emphasize marriage as a covenant-based union. A union, not simply between man and wife, but between a couple and God Almighty!

Introduction

One of my favorite sections in the newspaper is the People Page. I guess the reason I like it so much is that it is filled with smiling, happy people. Some of them are announcing their engagement, others a recent wedding, and still others are celebrating an anniversary milestone.

It makes my heart rejoice to see the excitement and optimism in each of their faces. Unfortunately, the reality of marriage today is tucked away in another section of the newspaper. It is there, in one column, you find the names of those happy people applying for marriage licenses. Next to it, in another column, is a list of people who are filing for divorce. This list is usually equal to if not longer than the list of those applying to get married.

The reality is that nearly 50% or more of those smiling faces on the People Page will end up in the "Filing for Divorce" column. Moreover, for those of you that think that 50% represents unchurched people... think again!

Traditional marriage is slowly being devalued and redefined by our culture! With more and more people choosing to live together before getting married, lobbyist groups attempting to redefine marriage to include more than just one man and one woman, and the relative ease of divorce, it is time that we begin to take seriously Hebrews 13:4 that states, "Marriage should be honored by all."

Maybe we would better understand the dilemma we are facing if we made divorcing couples put their pictures next to the "Filing for Divorce" column. That would be a "before and after" picture that would garner some attention.

Gone are the happy, smiling faces full of excitement and optimism. Those pictures have been replaced with photos of disillusioned and hurting people.

It is time that we begin to prepare people for a lifetime of commitment. We spend thousands of dollars, up to 4-8 years on a college education, to prepare ourselves for a career that many will only stay in for 5-10 years. If that is true, then what are we investing to prepare ourselves for a lifetime of commitment? The sad truth, is very little! Some people choose to get pre-marital counseling, but even that is not a requirement.

The problem we are facing is that marriage is simply seen as a legally binding agreement between two people. In reality, the One who instituted marriage in the Book of Genesis viewed marriage as a spiritual covenant. We should be ashamed if we view it any differently.

The first question that I ask every potential married couple is, "Why do you want to get married?" Although the answers vary in degree, the most common responses are: "Because we love each other"; "We want to spend the rest of our lives together;" or "We want to enjoy a deeper level of intimacy (which usually means sex)." What I am about to say next may shock you, but I tell them, "You don't need to get married." The fact is "culturally" speaking, you do not have to get married to love each other, live together forever, or have sex. All those things in our society are acceptable without getting married.

Inevitably, people will get to the heart of why they want to get married. They do not simply want a natural physical relationship. What they are searching for is a relationship with deeper meaning.

Most couples want to enjoy a natural and a spiritual relationship. This begs the question... Is marriage merely a legally binding agreement or is it a spiritual covenant?

The purpose of this book is to affirm that marriage, as established by God, is designed to be a spiritual covenant. With that in mind, we hope to prepare you, through careful study of God's Word, to enter into that very special union before God.

1

Covenant

A. LEGAL WEDDINGS OR SPIRITUAL UNIONS

Is marriage simply a legally binding agreement or is it a spiritual covenant? Is there a difference? If there is a difference, how then should we approach marriage, and how should we prepare for it?

Let us look together at Malachi 2:14 (NIV):

"You ask, "Why?" It is because the Lord is acting as a witness between you and the wife of your youth, because you have broken faith with her, though she is your partner, the wife of your marriage covenant."

What does this passage say about marriage? Is it simply a legally binding agreement or is it viewed as a covenant?

_____

Who does it say acts as witness to that covenant? _____

In Genesis 2:22-25 (NIV) God, Himself, instituted and presided over the very first marriage. Let us look at it together:

"Then the Lord God made a woman from the rib He had taken out of the man, and he brought her to the man. The man said, 'This is now bone of my bone and flesh of my flesh; she shall be called 'woman' for she was taken out of man.' For this reason a man will leave his father and mother and be united with his wife, and they will become one flesh. The man and his wife were both naked, and they felt no shame."

As the Father, bringing his daughter down the aisle to meet the groom, God brought Eve to Adam. It is here that for the first time the word "wife" is used indicating a union between Adam and Eve. She is now bone of his bone and flesh of his flesh. God, Himself, acted as the witness of the marriage covenant established between Himself, Adam and Eve. In the same way, God will be presiding as the witness over your marriage covenant!

B. WHAT IS A COVENANT?

In the minds of men and women today it is merely a "binding agreement." In contrast, throughout scripture, it was treated with much greater honor. It was upheld as an unbreakable commitment between individuals or peoples that provided for the mutual benefit of both. The significance is reflected in the sealing of the covenant in blood.

We see this in multiple places throughout the Old and New Testaments. Take time to read the following scriptures and answer the questions below.

1. In Genesis 15:1-21, whom did God establish a covenant with? _____

_____

2. Was the covenant sealed in blood? _____

3. In Exodus 12:1-28, with whom did God establish a covenant?

_____

4. What were they to place on the doorframes of their houses? _

_____

5. In Matthew 26:28, whom does Jesus establish a covenant with? _____

_____

6. What did he say "the cup" represented in this passage? _____

_____

We see that each covenant was initiated and instituted by God! The institution of marriage, as we have already seen, is also a covenant. However, it is not simply a covenant between a husband and wife. It is a covenant between "a couple" and the One who presides over their spiritual union ... God!

Malachi 2:15(NIV) states:

"Has not the Lord made them one? In flesh and spirit they are his. And why one? Because he was seeking godly offspring. So guard yourself in your spirit and do not break faith with the wife of your youth.

According to the passage above, what has the Lord made them?_____

_____

_____

They are one in _____ and _____.

As individuals they enter into covenant with each other, but as "one" they enter into covenant with God! When we marry, we enter into what I call the "Covenant Model." It is best described using the diagram below.

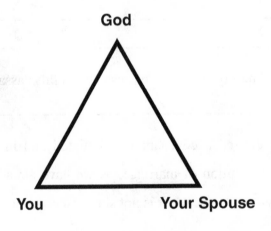

C. THE COVENANT MODEL

Take a moment to look at the diagram. Each of the lines represents an important facet of the marriage covenant. Each line represents a relationship. You have a relationship with God and a relationship with your spouse.

In the covenant model, who always occupies the top spot? _____

Matthew 22:37-39 (NIV) declares:

> *"Love the Lord your God with all your heart and with all your soul and with all your mind. This is the first and greatest commandment. And the second is like it: 'Love your neighbor as yourself."*

This makes the relationships between 'you and God' and 'your spouse and God' the most important relationships in your marriage. If they are healthy and strong, they will provide a covering over the relationship between you and your spouse.

Look back at the "Covenant Model" and see how your relationships with God form a nice tent-like covering, over your marriage at the bottom.

This model demonstrates that we not only have a natural relationship with each other, but we are to also have a spiritual relationship with God. In fact, structurally speaking, the bottom relationship is the least supportive. You can remove it and still maintain a tent-like structure. However, if you remove one of the relationships with God (the sides) from the structure, the whole covenant model collapses.

That is why 2 Corinthians 6:14 (NIV) declares:

"Do not be unequally yoked together with unbeliev-ers."

If you do not have a relationship with God, it will be impossible for the "covenant model" for marriage to stay healthy. This lays waste to some of the old adages we hear such as 'All we need is love,' or 'All we need is each other.' The most important thing you need is a strong, healthy relationship with the Lord.

Are you saved? Have you accepted Jesus Christ as the Lord and Savior of your life? Romans 10:9(NIV) declares:

"That if you confess with your mouth, 'Jesus is Lord,' and believe in your heart that God raised him from the dead, you will be saved."

You can begin a covenant relationship with God right now! Take a moment to pray and receive Jesus into your heart. You can pray this prayer and receive Jesus today:

Heavenly Father: I come to you today to ask for the forgiveness of my sins. I believe that Jesus is your Son and that He came and died on the cross for me. I realize the wages of sin is death and that Jesus died to pay the debt that I owed. I believe that on the third day that Jesus rose from the dead that I might have eternal life with Him and

I receive Him today as my Lord and Savior. Help me from this day on to live a life worthy of your Name. In Jesus Name. Amen.

Is having your own personal relationship with the Lord important to your marriage? Absolutely! Remember the covenant model? Without both partners having a strong, healthy relationship with the Lord, it jeopardizes the integrity of the marriage, and it also jeopardizes the "covering!"

D. THE COVENANT PROVIDES A COVERING

A covenant, as we defined it earlier, is an unbreakable commitment between two individuals that provides for the mutual benefit of both.

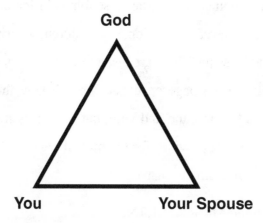

Let us take a moment to discover how we benefit from the marriage covenant. Notice from the visual how the relationship between 'you and God' and the relationship between 'your spouse and God' form a nice tent-like covering over the relationship between 'you and your spouse.'

1. Take a moment to write down some of the benefits that a married couple has compared to a single person or even an unmarried couple. _____

_____

_____

_____

_____

Some things, such as pre-marital sex, according to God's Word, are considered a sin. However, under the covering of the marriage covenant, sex is accepted and in fact even encouraged by God.

2. Now take a moment and write these things inside the covenant model you just viewed: protection, sex, children, security, spiritual intimacy, and blessing. These are just a few of the benefits that we enjoy within the marriage covenant. We see how the covenant model blesses the husband and wife, but how does it benefit the Lord? If a covenant provides for the mutual benefit of both, how does God benefit from our marriage?

Read with me Malachi 2:15(NIV):

"Has not the Lord made them one? In flesh and spirit they are his. And why one? Because He was seeking godly offspring"

3. According to this passage, why did God make them one?

God's benefit from our marriage covenant is "Godly off-spring." He desires for us to have children and to raise them in Godly homes: in fear and admonition of the Lord. This then establishes the validity of this covenant with both parties bene-fiting mutually from the sacred union.

Pastor's Note

Throughout the workbook, I have included this special section, "Pastor's Note," with just a thought or added scripture to emphasize the information covered in that chapter. Chapter one is packed with information and may warrant more than one counseling session. Its focal point, however, is on covenant and the covenant model of marriage. An additional scripture located in Proverbs 2:17(NIV) reinforces marriage, in God's eyes, as more than a legally binding agreement. The writer is speaking of an adulteress wife who has gone astray when he writes:

"Who (the wayward wife) has left the partner of her youth and ignored the covenant she made before God (Emphasis mine)."

Notice, she had come into a covenant before God! It is vital that every couple understands this, but it is even more important that every minister understand it. On their wedding day, they are striking a covenant with and before God. We must prepare them properly to enter that covenant.

NOTES

_____

_____

_____

_____

_____

_____

_____

_____

_____

_____

_____

_____

_____

_____

_____

_____

_____

_____

2

The Role of a Husband

A. BEFORE EVE

It is important to know that God did not just create two people and immediately bring them into the marriage covenant. Adam was an individual before God brought Eve into his life. A careful study of Genesis 1 & 2 shows us that God took careful measures to prepare Adam to lead a family. Let us look at some of those measures together:

1. Genesis 1:26, 27(NIV) tells us:

"Then God said, "Let us make man in our image, in our likeness, and let them rule over the fish of the sea and the birds of the air, over the livestock, over all the earth, and over all the creatures that move along the ground."

God made man in His _____ and _____.

> You, too, were created in God's image and likeness. Psalm 139:13-14(NIV) declares:
>
> *"For You created my inmost being; You knit me together in my mother's womb. I praise you because I am fearfully and wonderfully made."*
>
> You were created by God and for God! You are precious in His sight.

2. A careful reading of Genesis 2:1-20 shows us that before Adam had a "wife and kids,' he had his own relationship with God. I cannot emphasize enough, to the married and unmarried alike, that your individual relationship with God is the most important relationship you will ever have.

3. Genesis 2:8-15(NIV) tells us that Adam had a job! In fact, it was one of the first things that God gave him. Let's look at verse 15 together:

> *"The Lord God took the man and put him in the Garden of Eden to _____ it and _____ _____ of it."*
>
> Here is a bit of advice to those men looking to get married. You do not need a wife until you have a job. You cannot provide for a family, if you cannot even provide for yourself!

4. Genesis 2:16 teaches us that God gave Adam freedom (free-will to be more specific) to choose to do right and follow His commands or to choose to do wrong.

And, then, God entrusted Adam with a helpmate.

This suitable helpmate, according to Genesis 2:22-25, was taken from his side and the two became one flesh. The scriptures say that they were both naked and without shame. In essence, they were, without sin.

Is being sinless a covenant requirement? How can two people come together when we have all sinned and come short of the glory of God? Simply this, those who put their trust in Jesus Christ have been cleansed by the Word of God. They are washed in the blood of Christ! When God sees a born-again believer…He sees the righteousness of Christ. These believers, spiritually speaking, are naked and without shame! That is why the "marriage covenant" is designed for believers.

It is the duty of the husband to have a healthy relationship with the Lord "prior" to entering into this covenant. In fact, all the Bible's directives on marriage are directed towards "believers." There are no separate marriage instructions for unbelievers. The strongest case in point is found in Ephesians 5:22-33(NIV).

"Wives, submit to your husbands as to the Lord. For the husband is the head of the wife as Christ is the head of the church, his body, of which he is the Savior. Now as the

church submits to Christ, so also wives should submit to their husbands in everything.

Husbands, love your wives, just as Christ loved the church and gave Himself up for her to make her holy, cleansing her by the washing with water through the Word, and to present her to Himself as a radiant church, without stain or wrinkle or any other blemish, but holy and blameless.

In this same way, husbands ought to love their wives as their own bodies. He who loves his wife loves himself. After all, no one ever hated his own body, but he feeds and cares for it, just as Christ does the church for we are members of his body. "For this reason a man will leave his father and mother and be united to his wife, and the two will become one flesh." This is a profound mystery- but I am talking about Christ and the church. However, each one of you also must love his wife as he loves himself, and the wife must respect her husband."

B. Priest and Prophet

Ephesians 5 is notably the strongest passage of scripture that teaches us how to live as husbands and wives. It is here that we will begin to present God's plan for husbands to be the "priest and prophet" of their homes.

Let us begin with a simple definition of a priest and a prophet:

A priest is a person who speaks to God on behalf of the people.

A prophet is a person who speaks to the people on behalf of God.

As husbands we will see that we are required not only to speak to God about our families, but also speak to our families about God and His Holy Word.

Let us look at Ephesians 5:25-28(NIV) together:

"Husbands, love your wives, just as Christ loved the church and gave Himself up for her to make her holy, cleansing her by the washing with water through the word, and to present her to Himself as a radiant church, without stain or wrinkle or any other blemish. In this same way, husbands ought to love their wives as their own bodies. He who loves his wife loves himself."

1. What is the first thing that husbands are instructed to do?

_____

We are not simply to just love our wives, but to love them "as Christ loved the church." We cannot love as "Christ loved the church" if we do not have our own relationship with Christ. Again, I emphasize, as I did in the last chapter, it is significant that every husband have his own personal relationship with Jesus Christ.

The reason for that is found in the first ten words of Ephesians 5:25. For a husband to be able to love his wife as Christ loved the church, he must first know how it is that Christ loved. Knowing the depths of God's love comes through having your own relationship with Him. It is not gleaned by reading a book, but by experiencing it in your own heart and life. That is why having a personal relationship with the Lord before entering the marriage covenant is so important. You know, going into the marriage, the depths of God's love and the sacrifice that He made because you have experienced it in your own life.

Many husbands believe that their primary role as a husband is to "provide and protect." Although, these are components of being a husband, it is not where God places His emphasis. In Ephesians 5, God places His emphasis on being a "priest and prophet." His first instruction to us is to "love our wives as Christ loved the church."

The question to be asked then is this: How did Christ love the church?

He did not do it with an occasional "I love you," or a box of candies, or a dozen roses! Rather, Romans 5:8 states that God demonstrated His love for us in this: *"While we were yet sinners, Christ died for us."*

2. What does Ephesians 5:25 say that Christ did to make her holy? _____

_____

Literally, He sacrificed Himself for her!

And so it is with godly husbands. We are to demonstrate our love by "giving ourselves up" for her! That means that we may have to give up some of what we want in order to accomplish the will of God in our marriages.

This type of sacrificial giving of ourselves, in obedience to God's Word, is not the common practice in our society. It does not come natural to us; in fact, your flesh will certainly oppose it, your family will surely question it, and your friends may criticize you for it. However, what it will accomplish in your marriage will certainly be worth the effort. What is it then that we are looking to accomplish through our sacrificial giving?

Ephesians 5:26 states that Christ sacrificed Himself for the church in order to "make her holy"! (Not to make her happy, to satisfy the in-laws, or to make ourselves look better than the guy next to us) He sacrificed Himself to make her holy. To be holy is to be set apart unto God for His purposes. Christ gave of Himself so we, as believers, would be set apart unto God.

Husbands, as priests and prophets, are called to be the spiritual leaders of their homes. It is their responsibility to see their families "set apart unto God." This begins with our wives.

Christ cleansed the church by the washing with water through the Word. We then, like Christ, must also bathe our wives and families in the Word of God. God places a high value on the soul and spirit of a person. That is why being priest and prophet is of such importance. That doesn't mean that being a good provider is not important, but what does Mark 8:36 say about it?

3. What does it profit a man to gain the whole world yet lose his own soul? _____

We must take our role as priest and prophet seriously. It is not only the man's soul that is at risk, but his families as well.

According to Ephesians 5:27 Christ wanted to present to Himself a radiant church. A radiant church is one without stain or wrinkle or any blemish, but holy and blameless. The church, when presented, would be a direct reflection of His love and sacrifice. The extent that He invested in her would be immediately noticeable. As a husband, our wives are a reflection of our love and sacrifice.

4. Is your love and sacrifice noticeable? _____

It should be every husband's desire to see his wife and family grow in their relationships with Jesus Christ. Godly families, however, do not happen by accident. They happen on purpose! They develop when Godly husbands and fathers, learn to sacrifice of themselves to help their families grow in their faith.

C. Provider and Protector

Unfortunately for many families, husbands have adopted a philosophy that if they bring home a paycheck then they have fulfilled their duties as a husband. Although providing for our families is of the utmost importance, it is curious that God does not place much emphasis on it in Ephesians 5.

> *"In this same way, husbands ought to love their wives as their own bodies. He who loves his wife loves himself. After all, no one ever hated his own body, but he feeds and cares for it, just as Christ does the church."*

> Ephesians 5:28-29(NIV)

"Feeding and caring" is directly correlated to "providing and protecting." What God goes on to say is very interesting! Remember, in Genesis, God gave Adam a job, 'to provide for himself,' before he gave him a wife. You going to work each day to bring home a paycheck is something you would do even if you did not have a wife. You would work in order to feed and care for yourself.

What makes this fact more significant when you get a wife?

_____

_____

She is now bone of your bone, flesh of your flesh… you are still providing for "You." The "You" is now you and your spouse because you are one flesh.

The role of "Provider and Protector" is important, but it is also natural. "Priest and Prophet," however, require a sacrifice from you! This sacrificial living is not just instructed to you, but it is expected from you because of your position as head of the home.

D. HUSBANDS AND HEADSHIP

"Now I want you to realize that the head of every man is Christ, and the head of the woman is man, and the head of Christ is God."

1 Corinthians 11:3(NIV)

Most men embrace the idea that "the head of the woman is man" and then neglect the rest. They tend to forget that the head of Christ is God and the head of man is Christ. When it comes to being the head of your homes, it is not knowing who you are head over that is important, but it is knowing who you are under!

You must first know what it means to submit to the headship of another if you expect others to submit to your headship! Look at the emphasis I have underlined here in Ephesians 5:23(NIV):

"For the husband is head of the wife <u>as Christ is the head of the church,</u> his body, of which he is the Savior."

Who are you learning headship from? _____

If it is not Jesus Christ, then you will struggle, for as we just read in 1 Corinthians 11:3, Christ is the head of man.

Therefore, what can we learn from Jesus that will help us to lead our families?

a. To begin with, Jesus did not bark out orders, demand self-ishly or expect to be waited on hand and foot.

b. Jesus demonstrated headship by being a servant to the church. He donned an apron and washed the disciples feet, He spoke words of comfort and encouragement, He laid hands on the sick, He prayed for people, He taught them God's Word, He fed them physically, He protected them from the storm, and when it was tax time, He did that too.

c. Matthew 20:28(NIV) tells us: *"The Son of man did not come to be served, but to serve, and give His life as a ransom for many."*

The, "I'll do as I please attitude," that prevails in most homes is not the example provided for us by Jesus. In John 5:19-20(NIV), Jesus says;

"I tell you the truth, the Son can do nothing by Him-self; He can do only what He sees His Father doing, because whatever the Father does the Son also does. For the Father loves the Son and shows Him all He does. Yes, to your amazement He will show Him even greater things than these."

That is precisely why Jesus came…to show us how to live! If we truly desire to succeed as husbands, then we must examine the model of Christ and do as He did.

Pastor's Note

Author and speaker, Rev. Wellington Boone, spoke at a Promise Keepers Conference several years ago which I had the privilege of attending. I cannot tell you who else spoke at that particular conference or what they spoke about. The one thing that I do remember was this one quote from Wellington Boone and this is it: "I refuse to let my wife out serve me!" When I heard it, I thought to myself; "That is what I want to be as a husband." When I got home, I realized just how hard it is to actually do it! By no means, have I perfected being a husband, but one thing I know, Jesus is the head of this man! He is my example and everyday we ought to strive to do as we see Him do. It is time that we viewed headship from its proper perspective. Headship is a place of service and sacrifice!

NOTES

_____

_____

_____

_____

_____

_____

_____

_____

_____

_____

_____

_____

_____

_____

_____

_____

_____

_____

_____

_____

_____

3

The Role of a Wife

"A wife of noble character who can find? She is worth far more than rubies."

Proverbs 31:10(NIV)

As the old adage goes, "It takes two to tango," so it is true in marriage. We have spent some time looking at the husbands in this equation, but now we turn our attention to the wives. Proverbs 18:22(NIV) declares:

"He who finds a wife finds what is good and receives favor from the Lord."

I believe that it is the desire of most men to find a wife, not just any wife, but a wife of noble character. So let us look to the beginning and see God's intention for the godly wife and woman.

A. WHILE YOU WERE SLEEPING!

When we once again look at the book of Genesis, we find some striking similarities that we cannot overlook.

1. First, Genesis 1:27(NIV) tells us:

   "So God created man in his own image, in the image of God he created him; male and female he created them."

   Therefore, like the man, she bears in herself the image and likeness of God.

2. She also had a relationship with God before He brought her to the man. The extent of that relationship is unknown, but we can be certain that once God created her ... she had knowledge of her creator.

3. Like the man, according to Genesis 2:26 and 3:2 she was given the freedom to *choose to do right* and follow God's commands or *choose to do wrong*.

4. As we read in Genesis 1:26(NIV), she also had responsibility!

   "Then God said, "Let us make man in our image, in our likeness, and let them rule over the fish of the sea and the birds of the air, over the livestock, over all the earth, and over all the creatures that move along the ground."

   Verse 28 tells us that God blessed them and said to them' "be fruitful and increase in number, fill the earth and subdue it." Then he told them to, "rule over all the fish, birds and every living creature."

5. Lastly, she too was naked and without shame according to Genesis 2:25.

It is clear that it is the duty of every wife, as it is the duty of every husband, to have a healthy relationship with God prior to entering into the marriage covenant. Why is it important to be born-again? The answer to that question is…wholeness!

B. You Do Not Complete Me!

There is a line in the movie "Jerry Maquire," that is part of the climactic love scene at the end of the movie, in which Jerry tells his wife, "You complete me"! Although touching to watch, the idea that is sent to couples is very dangerous.

1. The idea that having someone or a certain person in your life will bring wholeness or completion is misleading.

2. When we do this we set the other person up immediately to fail, because no one can bring wholeness to a person, except Jesus Christ! The idea of having a "better half" means there is now an expectation for that person to have the stronger character in your relationship.

3. Before God brought Eve to Adam they were both "complete." God brought two "whole" people together and they

became one flesh. There was not anything intrinsically lacking in either one of them that would have required something in the other person to meet. They were whole and
complete because of their relationship with God. In fact,
Genesis 1:31 states that God looked upon all that He made
and declared it was good. He did not create them lacking in
any way.

Why then did God create Eve and bring her to Adam? _____

_____

Let us look at Genesis 2:19-20(NIV):

*"Now the Lord God had formed out of the ground all
the beasts of the field and all the birds of the air. He
brought them to the man to see what he would name them;
and whatever the man called each living creature, that
was its name. So the man gave names to all the livestock,
the birds of the air and all the beasts in the field. But for
Adam no suitable helper was found."*

4. God brought Eve to Adam, not for completeness, but for
   companionship! No suitable helper had been found, so God
   created another of Adam's kind to be his helpmate. If you
   are looking for a mate, stop looking for one to fill the voids
   in your life. Look to God to do that! Let God make you
   whole, and pray that He would send you a suitable helpmate.

Wholeness begins with a "healthy" relationship with Jesus Christ. This relationship is foundational to your marriage. God's instruction to women on being godly wives, recorded in Ephesians 5, is rooted in your relationship with Christ.

Let us look at this together:

"Wives, submit to your husbands as to the Lord."

Ephesians 5:22(NIV)

Before a wife can submit to her husband "as to the Lord," she must first know what it means to submit to the lordship of Jesus Christ. Look at verse 24 below:

"Now as the church submits to Christ, also wives should submit to their husbands."

Ephesians 5:24

This verse could not be understood aside from having a relationship with Christ. A woman who does not know what it means to submit unto Christ cannot properly submit to her husband.

What then does it mean to be submitted to your spouse? _____

_____

C. THE ART OF GODLY SUBMISSION

The act of godly submission is an art form. More specifically, it is a rare art form. You know what I mean, the kind that you rarely find and only read about in books. However, like rare art, it is also priceless. The value that true submission brings to a marriage is incalculable. So valuable is it, in fact, that God makes it virtually the entire source of His instruction to women in Ephesians 5. Let us look at it together:

> *"Wives, submit to your husbands as to the Lord. For the husband is the head of the wife as Christ is the head of the church, his body, of which he is the Savior. Now as the church submits to Christ, so also wives should submit to their husbands in everything."*

Ephesians 5:22-24(NIV)

I recently heard a Focus on the Family broadcast about men and women. That day's speaker posed a question to an audience at an event at which he had recently spoken. He asked them, "Would you rather go through life feeling unloved or inadequate"? The speaker said that 95% of the women replied that they would rather feel inadequate, and 95% of the men said they would rather feel unloved. Although this is just one man's testimony from one event, it mirrors what God is teaching us in Ephesians 5!

> *"However, each one of you also must love his wife as he loves himself, and the wife must respect her husband."*

Ephesians 5:33(NIV)

Women want to be loved and men want to be respected. Just as love is demonstrated through sacrifice and service, respect is demonstrated through submission.

1. What is biblical submission?

    a. Submission is to *willfully commit to the discretion and decision of another.* It is a willful decision, not a mandate! The wife chooses to commit to the discretion and decision of her husband.

    (Special note to the husbands: Submission does not equal lordship! You cannot force your wife to submit anymore than she can force you to love her by "giving yourself" up for her. Both are willful actions that are tied to our relationship with Christ. We are to love out of our love and obedience to Christ, and we are to submit out of our love and obedience to Christ.)

    b. Something important to notice is that these scriptures are not conditional. You cannot say, "If she shows me respect, then I will love her." You are to love her because of your relationship with Christ. Moreover, wives cannot say, "If he loves me, then I'll respect and submit to him." You are to submit to him because of your relationship with Christ. You are not submitting out of a reverence for your husband, but rather out of your reverence for God!

2. A common problem in marriages!

a. Let's take a moment to address a common problem in many marriages. 1 Corinthians 11:3 reads, *"Now I want you to realize that the head of every man is Christ, and the head of the woman is man, and the head of Christ is God."* As long as the husband stays under the headship of Christ, then he maintains the position of headship over his home. When he comes out from under the headship of Christ then he in essence is abandoning the spiritual headship of his household.

b. Here is where the problem arises. Many times, the wife will attempt to function as the head of the home. Wives, if your husband abandons his role as the spiritual head of your home, it does not default to you.

c. The role of headship still belongs to your husband even if he is not functioning in it. What happens is it becomes very difficult when the husband later steps back under the headship of Christ to then reassume his position as head of the home when his wife is unwilling to submit. She is unwilling to submit because she has in essence been the "acting head of the home."

A husband's unwillingness to lead, unwillingness to love, and unwillingness to live for Christ are not an excuse for the wife not to submit. As long as it does not contradict God's Word or your safety… submit!

"Wives, in the same way be submissive to your husbands so that, if any of them do not believe the word, they may be won over without words by the behavior of their wives, when they see the purity and reverence of your lives. Your beauty should not come from outward adornment, such as braided hair and the wearing of gold jewelry and fine clothes. Instead, it should be that of your

inner self, the unfading beauty of a gentle and quiet spirit, which is of great worth in God's sight.

For this is the way the holy women of the past who put their hope in God used to make themselves beautiful. They were submissive to their own husbands, like Sarah, who obeyed Abraham and called him her master. You are her daughters if you do what is right and do not give way to fear."

1 Peter 3:1-6(NIV)

1. This passage of text instructs wives who have husbands that "do not believe the Word" to be submissive, so they (the unbelieving husband) may be won over without talk by the behavior of their wives.

2. This type of obedience to God's word is like a beautiful adornment. Verse 6 states that it is the unfading beauty of a gentle spirit that is of great worth in God's sight.

3. It is the way that the holy women of the past, who put their hope in God, used to make themselves beautiful...they were submissive to their husbands.

Reclaim the lost art of submission in your home and teach it to your daughters. Titus 2:4-5 instructs the older women to teach the younger women how to be submissive to their husbands, so that no one will malign the word of God. Remember the act of submission is willful and is to be exercised out of your love and reverence for God!

Pastor's Note

Titus 2:3-5 and Proverbs 31:10-31 are excellent passages of scripture for further study. I encourage the ladies looking to get married and even those who are already married to spend some time studying these scriptures. If they are serious about becoming wives of noble character then this is a great place to start.

NOTES

_____

_____

_____

_____

_____

4

Communication

"For everyone who asks receives, he who seeks finds, and to him who knocks the door is open."

Matthew 7:8(NIV)

Communication is the number one cause of difficulties between married couples. Finances and infidelity are right behind, but even they often stem from a lack of communication. Before we can begin to approach this topic, we must establish two ground rules:

Ground Rule #1: You are not a mind reader!

Ground Rule #2: Your spouse is not a mind reader!

If you want your spouse to know your wants, needs and desires then you are going to have to "communicate" with them. The second part of James 4:2(NIV) states:

"You do not have, because you do not ask God."

Take a moment to read Matthew 6:8.

Although our God knows our needs, what does He require us to do?

Please do not hold your spouse to a higher standard than God holds you. Do not just expect them to know your needs and respond. God, who is all-knowing and all-powerful, is keenly aware of your needs, and He still requires you to communicate with Him.

So what is communication?

A. COMMUNICATION DEFINED

1. Simply defined: It is the exchange of information between individuals. Note specifically the word "exchange"! This means that it is not one-sided. You telling your spouse…"This is what we are going to do"…is not communication. That is information.

2. There are two types of communication that we must look at:

Healthy: which is full of grace, respect, truth and love.

Unhealthy: which is demanding, forceful and self-seeking.

"The tongue has the power of life and death, and those who love it will eat its fruit."

Proverbs 18:21(NIV)

The life and death of your marriage is found there as well!

B. LISTENING IS THE KEY TO SPEAKING!

1. James 1:19(NIV) states that everyone should be quick to listen slow to speak, and slow to become angry. The key to good communication is not found in great speaking, but in great listening.

2. Proverbs 1:5(NIV) states:
    "Let the wise _____ and add to their learning."

3. Proverbs 18:13(NIV) says,
    "He who answers before listening, that is _____."

We ought to approach conversations with our spouses in much the same way that Solomon approached God in conversation. Let us look together at Ecclesiastes 5:1-3(NIV):

"Guard your steps when you go to the house of God. Go near to listen rather than to offer the sacrifice of fools, who do not know that they do wrong. Do not be quick with your mouth; do not be hasty in your heart to utter any-

thing before God. God is in heaven and you are on earth, so let your words be few. As a dream comes when there are many cares, so the speech of a fool when there are many words."

There are some key elements from this single passage that we can apply in our marriages.

a. Go near to listen! Fights often begin because we blaze into a conversation to defend ourselves without truly listening to the grievance. We become hasty in our hearts and begin to make assumptions that are unfounded because we do not want to take the time to listen.

b. This leads us to be quick with our mouths. It is an attempt to make sure that we get our "verbal punches" in before we look like fools. This is amusing considering Solomon called the use of many words the "sacrifice of fools."

Look up Luke 6:45 and write below the last sentence of that verse:

_____

_____

When you speak in haste, you reveal your heart! So many times people say things that they wish they could take back. They reveal things that they hoped not to divulge. I guess the old adage applies here...better to look like a fool, rather than actually be one.

c. Lastly, he said, "So let your words be few." Choose your words wisely. Words have the power of life and death in them. They have the power to build up and to tear down. Look up the following verse: Proverbs17:27(NIV). If we are going to exercise wisdom when we speak ...How then should we speak?

4. Basic guidelines by which to live: (See if you can pick out the principal behind each verse.)

   a. Proverbs 22:11(NIV)

   _____

   _____

   _____

   Our conversation should be full of grace. Grace is unmerited favor. Strive to speak words that build up, encourage, and strengthen.

   b. Colossians 4:6(NIV)

   _____

   _____

   _____

   This is tact! Tact is always truthful, but it is salted so that it is easier to swallow. It is a keen sense of knowing what to say to maintain good relations with others while upholding truth.

Ephesians 4:15(NIV)

_____

_____

_____

c. Our conversations should be motivated by love. It has
been said, "No one cares how much you know, until
they know how much you care." What motivates your
conversations? Is it simply a desire to see your own
needs met? Do you approach every conversation with
battle armor on... ready to defend yourself? Or do you
come to the table with a heart that desires to grow in
intimacy with your spouse?

d. Matthew 5:37(NIV)

_____

_____

_____

Simply let your "yes" be "yes" and let your "no" be
"no." Anything beyond this comes from the evil one.
There is no place for white lies or half-truths in marriage.

e. Malachi 2:16(NIV)

_____

_____

_____

This passage points out that God hates divorce and He hates a man that covers himself/his spouse with violence. Verbal abuse indicates a spiritual problem with the abuser and often precedes physical abuse. Your marriage is in immediate need of help if this should creep in.

Communication in a marriage should always be deliberate, open, often, and filled with respect.

NOTES

_____

_____

_____

_____

_____

_____

_____

_____

_____

_____

5

Biblical Finances

"The earth is the Lord's and everything in it, the world, and all who live in it; for he founded it upon the seas and established it upon the waters."

Psalm 24:1-2(NIV)

A. THE INITIAL PREMISE

The majority of the problems that individuals and couples face in regards to finances are rooted in the fact that their "initial premise" is wrong. Let me give you an exaggerated example.

You and your family plan a wonderful trip to Florida for vacation. Now, you have never been to Florida, but many people have told you that Florida is just north of Michigan. If you operate from this initial premise, most of your decisions after this will be futile, as you will soon find out upon reaching Canada!

Psalm 24, above, lays out for us the initial premise we must operate from when considering biblical finances. That premise is this: "You do not own anything!"

You may possess it, but everything belongs to God. 100% of everything you have and receive belongs to Him.

Look up and write down Colossians 1:16. _____

_____

_____

_____

_____

_____

Problems arise when we begin to lay claim to things, which belong to God, as our own. It is only when we begin to view ourselves as "stewards" of God's riches that we begin to enjoy a healthy perspective of money and wealth.

B. STEWARDSHIP

The Bible talks about many things of which we have been entrusted as believers. We have been entrusted with the message of hope, the love of God, gifts and talents, and yes, even wealth. The Bible also says in 1 Corinthians 4:2 that it is required of those who have been given a trust to prove faithful.

1. Arguably, the most well known scripture on being faithful with God's possessions is found in Matthew 25. It is known as the parable of the talents.

Take a few moments and read Matthew 25:14-30. Then copy verse 14 in the space below: _____

_____

_____

Did you notice our "initial premise" woven in this opening verse?

As you have just read:

a. He entrusted his property in various measures to his servants. Some received two, some five, and some ten talents. Notice that he did not give them his talents or entrust them with their own wealth. He entrusted them with 100% of his own property.

b. Then after a long time he returned to settle accounts with them. Many people believe that they have fulfilled their obligation towards God as long as they have given weekly in the church offering. That would be true if God only cared about the tithe. One day, we will not simply stand before God for what we did with the 10% (the tithe), but what we did with the remaining 90% as well. God will settle all His accounts.

    c. The basic principal we find in Matthew 25 is that those who are faithful, with all of God's property given to them, will be given more and those who are not will have even what they were given taken away. Stewardship then becomes a lifestyle, not just a Sunday morning event.

2. In another story, found in Luke 12:42-47, the Bible describes a faithful and wise steward as one who takes what has been entrusted and "gives" at the proper times.
He is the one the master finds doing His will when He returns. However, Luke also gives us a strong warning about the steward that misuses the master's riches.

    a. The master's riches were to be used to help others, but instead the steward mistreated the people and used the riches on himself!

    b. Verse 46 states that the master will come and deal ever so severely with that unwise servant.

    c. The basic principle of Luke 12 is summed up in verse 48(NIV):

"From everyone given much, much will be demanded; and from the one who has been entrusted with much, much more will be asked."

Some have said that this life is a test run for the life to come. If He cannot trust you with "worldly wealth" how can He trust you with true riches in the age to come? That is precisely what stewardship is … a matter of trust, but it is not a matter of trust on God's part as it is a matter of trust on ours.

C. A MATTER OF TRUST

Do you believe that as you are faithful with God's riches that He will take care of you? _____

_____

Your answer to that question will determine how good of a steward that you are going to be. If you believe that God does not have enough to take care of you and Himself, then you are going to mishandle what He gives you. Remember a good steward, as we read in Luke 12, is one who knows and does the master's will.

In fact, this is the same principal taught to us in the Old Testament book of Deuteronomy.

Take a moment to look up Deuteronomy 28 and read verses 1-14. Then copy verse two in the space provided below:

_____
_____
_____
_____
_____

A careful reading of verses 1-28 reinforces God's will to bless those, who obey His commands with success, protection and abundant prosperity.

Now take a moment to look up and read Deuteronomy 28:15-29. Then copy verse 15 in the space provided below:

_____

_____

_____

_____

The remainder of the chapter records the consequences and curses of being disobedient. If you will trust God and obey His commands...success and prosperity are assured. When we stop doing His will and attempt to manage things our own way we can be certain that disappointment and destruction will follow.

With this in mind, we ought to know what the Bible says about wealth and finances if we are going to be obedient in doing it.

D. THREE BIBLICAL DYNAMICS

When discussing finances, we can approach the topic from two directions. One is from a practical standpoint, which can include budgeting, bill paying, balancing a checkbook and goal setting. The other is a biblical standpoint. When it comes to biblical finances, we can narrow our discussion down to basically three dynamics. Those three dynamics are giving, borrowing, and saving.

(We will discuss more on practical finances in the "Pastor's Note" at the end of this chapter.)

Remembering that God blesses our obedience, let us see what God has to say about giving.

1. Giving & Tithing

"Remember this: Whoever sows sparingly will also reap sparingly, and whoever sows generously will also reap generously. Each man should give what he has decided in his heart to give, not reluctantly or under compulsion, for God loves a cheerful giver"

2 Corinthians 9: 6-7(NIV)

a. Giving

It is evident from this passage of scripture that our blessing is tied to our giving. If we give sparingly then we will receive sparingly. If we give generously, then we will receive generously.

Take a moment to read verses 8-11.

What does verse eight say that God is able to make abound to you? _____

_____

What is grace? It is God's unmerited favor towards man. As you give, God makes His unmerited favor abound towards you.

Why, according to verse 8, does He do this? _____

_____

_____

_____

There will be some of you who read this that will say: "But I don't have enough to give and still put bread on the table." Remember, stewardship is a matter of trust.

Take a moment now and read 2 Corinthians 9:10 and then copy in the space provided below:_____

_____

_____

_____

_____

Seed is what you sow into other people's lives! Bread is what you consume.

God says that when you give He will not only supply you with more seed to sow, but with bread to eat as well. Your needs will be met when you are obedient to give according to God's Word.

Why is your giving so important? (Look to verse 11) _____

_____

_____

_____

Your generosity will result in thanksgiving to God! This is
precisely what Jesus said in Matthew 5:16 ... *"In the same way,
let your light shine before men, that they may see your good
deeds and praise your Father in heaven."*

   b. Tithing

Is giving the same thing as tithing? _____

Giving is a heart issue. Tithing is an act of obedience
and worship. Giving goes far beyond a regulated per-
centage. Where did tithing get its start? Tithing was
introduced in the Old Testament when Abraham brought
the King of Salem, Melchizidek, 10% of his spoils from
battle to honor the Lord.

We see the principle reinforced in Genesis 28:22. Read
and copy this passage below: _____

_____

_____

_____

_____

Here Jacob makes a vow to God saying that if God would be
with him, watch over him, give him food to eat and clothes to
wear, and grant him safe return to his father's house, then he

would give back to God a tenth of all that He gave into his hands. Jacob understood that it all belonged to God and trusted God for his own provision.

Take a moment to read for yourselves these additional references on tithing:

Leviticus 27:30

Numbers 18:21

Deuteronomy 12:6

Let us also look at one final scripture found in Malachi 3:10(NIV):

> *"Bring the whole tithe into the storehouse, that there*
> *may be food in my house. 'Test me in this,' says the Lord*
> *Almighty, 'and see if I will not throw open the floodgates*
> *of heaven and pour out so much blessing that you will not*
> *have room enough for it."*

Remember, we are stewards over 100% of what God gives us. People's reluctance to bring their tithe into the storehouse is often due to a mishandling of the other 90%. As a Christian, I bring in the tithe in obedience to God's Word. It is the firstfruits of all that God has provided me.

> *"Honor the Lord with your wealth, with the firstfruits*
> *of all your crops; then your barns will be filled to over-*
> *flowing, and your vats will brim over with new wine"*
>
> Proverbs 3:9-10(NIV)

My giving, although, does not end there. I am still then responsible to give out of the 90%, as the Lord directs me, to help meet the needs of others. In a manner of speaking, I am trusting God to do more with the 90% that remains, than I could have done with the entire 100%.

The dilemma we face today is that we consume not just 100% of what we get, but often more than we receive. Our society's fascination with debt has hindered our ability to give. We are consuming not only the bread that God has provided, but we are devouring the seed too! Without having seed to sow ... we will not be able to reap!

2. Borrowing

"The rich rule over the poor, and the borrower is servant to the lender,"

Proverbs 22:7(NIV)

Is debt a sin? _____

The answer to that is "not necessarily." If, however, your debt hinders you from being obedient to the Word of God, then the answer is absolutely! Borrowing puts us in an unfavorable position with another person or entity. When we incur debt, we obligate ourselves to repaying that debt and in turn obligate ourselves to that other person.

Borrowing has become so common in our society that most people probably do not see themselves as "servants to their lenders." However, be assured, should you miss paying for two or three months, your opinion will soon change as they tow away your car and foreclose on your home.

God's Word is clear that borrowing is not God's intention for His people!

Let us look at two contrasting scriptures from Deuteronomy 28:

> *"The Lord will open the heavens, the storehouse of his bounty, to send rain on your land in season and to bless all the work of your hand. You will lend to many nations but will borrow from none."*

Deuteronomy 28:12(NIV)

> *"The alien who lives among you will rise above you higher and higher, but you will sink lower and lower. He will lend to you, but you will not lend to him. He will be the head, but you will be the tail.*

Deuteronomy 28:43-44(NIV)

If we are obedient to God's Word, then we will live in abundance and prosperity. When we live in disobedience to God's Word and mishandle what He has given us, we find ourselves having to borrow. When we borrow continually, we subject ourselves to the headship of the lender. We move ourselves out of the blessing column and into the cursing column.

Borrowing does not simply include debt that you incur directly, but debt that you co-sign for as well. "You mean the Bible talks about co-signing a loan?" Absolutely!

Look up Proverbs 17:18 and copy it on the space provided below:

_____

_____

_____

Also, Proverbs 11:15: _____

_____

_____

According to Proverbs 6:1-5 this type of debt is described as a trap!

"My son, if you have put up security for your neighbor, if you have struck hands in pledge for another, if you have been trapped by what you said, ensnared by the words of your mouth, then do this, my son, to free yourself, since you have fallen into your neighbor's hands: Go and humble yourself; press your plea with your neighbor! Allow no sleep to your eyes, no slumber to your eyelids. Free yourself, like a gazelle, from the hand of the fowler."

Clearly, when we find ourselves in debt, we are not to continue to amass more debt. We are to work to free ourselves from this snare! In fact, Romans 13:8 tells us the only debt that we are to have is the continuing debt of love one to another.

The only thing that rivals how much debt that we have is how little we have saved!

3. Savings

"A good man leaves an inheritance for his children's children, but a sinner's wealth is stored up for the righteous."

Proverbs 13:22(NIV)

How am I going to leave my children's children an inheritance if I can barely make my minimum payments?

It starts by freeing yourself from the hand of the fowler. Get out of debt! Proverbs 6:6-8(NIV) goes on to tell us how to hold the "debt master" at bay!

"Go to the ant, you sluggard; consider its ways and be wise! It has no commander, no overseer or ruler, yet it stores its provisions in summer and gathers its food at harvest."

Winter will come. So be prepared. Start putting something back. Be ready for those unforeseen expenses. If you do not, you will find yourself at the door of the lender once again.

The Flip Side:

Is it possible to store up wealth in a way that is unhealthy?_____

Take a moment to read Luke 12:13-21. Here we are told a story of a man who produced a good crop. So good in fact, that he did not have room enough to store all of his crops. Therefore, he decided to tear down his barns and build bigger ones to hold all his wealth. He was then going to take life easy, eat, drink and be merry. Apparently, he never considered using those resources to help others. He simply stored up wealth for himself. That night his life was demanded of him. Jesus asked, "Then who will get what you have prepared for yourself? This is how it will be with anyone who stores up things for himself but is not rich towards God."

We must strike up a healthy balance. We should store up enough to be prepared, but not so much that we begin to trust in riches more than we trust in God.

Look up Luke 16:13. What does Jesus say about trusting in riches?

_____

_____

You are either moved by your finances or moved by God! The question you have to ask yourself is: Do you believe that if you are faithful with God's riches that He will take care of you?

Pastor's Note

It is important that we provide potential couples with not only the biblical foundation, but also the practical application for financial success. We have found great success with the "Total Money Makeover" material written by financial author Dave Ramsey. We do a practical session where we help the couple develop a budget and discuss Dave Ramsey's established "7-Baby Steps." Mr. Ramsey's principals are Bible-based and compliment the teaching that your couple has just received. As part of the "Total Money Makeover" program, there is also a 13-week class available that empowers and teaches you how to make the right money decisions to achieve your financial goals. This might be an awesome addition to your regular pre-marital counseling sessions. For more information about the Dave Ramsey programs listed: The Total Money Makeover, Financial Peace University, and the 7-Baby Steps visit his website at daveramsey.com.

NOTES

_____

_____

6

Keep the Marriage Bed Pure

"Marriage should be honored by all, and the marriage bed kept pure, for God will judge the adulterer and all the sexually immoral."

Hebrews 13:4(NIV)

A. KEEP IT CONTAINED

I heard a wise person once describe sex like this: "Sex is like a fire. In a fireplace, it's warm and delightful. Outside the hearth, it's destructive and uncontrollable." Sex within the covering of the marriage covenant is a beautiful and fulfilling experience. Unfortunately, the idea of sex has gone to two extremes: "If it feels good do it!" Or "It's simply for procreation"

1. The key is a healthy balance and a proper understanding of covenant. It is important for us to know that as a part of our marriage covenant that God desires "godly offspring."

> *"Has not the Lord, made them one? In flesh and in spirit they are his. And why one? Because he was seeking godly offspring."*

> Malachi 2:15(NIV)

2. It is also important to know that this is not the only place that God talks about sex. The Song of Solomon shows us that sex was not confined merely to procreation. It was also established as a way to create deeper intimacy between husbands and wives.

We therefore honor our marriage and spouse when we strive to keep the marriage bed pure. Let us look together again at Hebrews 13:4 above. There are two classes of people who will be judged for "defiling" the marriage bed.

Who are they? _____ and _____.

B. SEXUAL IMMORALITY

1. IT IS GOD'S WILL THAT YOU AVOID SEXUAL IMMORALITY

In 1 Timothy 5:22 the Apostle Paul charges Timothy and the other church leaders to keep themselves pure. This lends itself nicely here so that the best way to keep the marriage bed pure is to first keep yourself pure. This begins with a basic understanding of Romans 6:13(NIV):

"Do not offer the parts of your body to sin, as instruments of wickedness, but rather offer yourselves to God as those who have been brought from death to life; and offer the parts of your body to him as instruments of righteousness."

Many of you may be thinking, "Surely, whenever Paul wrote this he wasn't associating it with sex." A careful study of Romans 6 will reveal that Paul's focus is on dying to sin... more precisely to the sin nature.

Take a few minutes to read the following scripture verses:

Galatians 5:19

Ephesians 5:3

Colossians 3:5

1 Thessalonians 4:3

What does every one of these passages list as the first thing that should be put to death of the old sin nature? _____

_____

1 Thessalonians 4:3-4(NIV) is especially vivid:

"It is God's will that you should be holy; that you should avoid sexual immorality: that each of you should learn to control his own body in a way holy and honorable."

2. YOUR BODY IS MEANT FOR THE LORD

Paul's most direct response to sexual immorality is found in 1 Corinthians 6:12-20(NIV). This passage can be summed up in verse 13. Look up 1 Corinthians 6 and copy verse 13 below: _____

_____

_____

_____

As part of our marriage covenants, we do not avoid "sexual immorality" simply for the sake of our spouse. We do it for the Lord! You see, verse 15, in the above passage states that your bodies are members of Christ Himself. "Shall you then take the members of Christ and unite them with a prostitute?"

When we participate in sexual immorality, as believers, we subject Christ to it! This is why, in verse 18, Paul pleads for us to flee sexual immorality.

"All other sins a man commits are outside the body, but he who sins sexually, sins against his own body."

It is true that all sin is destructive, but sexual sin destroys body, soul and spirit!

Remember, you are not your own, you were bought with a price.

What does verse 19 say then we are to do with our bodies?

_____

3. WHAT DOES SEXUAL IMMORALITY INCLUDE

Let us discuss some terms you will read in scripture and define them as simply as possible.

a. Fornication: is having sex outside of the marriage covenant. Today it can be known as "hooking up" or "friends with benefits," however you package it, it is still sexual sin.

b. Adultery: is having sex with anyone, other than the husband or wife of your marriage covenant.

c. Homosexuality: is having sexual relations with a member of the same sex. You may see those who participate in this referred to as sodomites throughout scripture.

d. Prostitution: is selling your body, for the purposes of sex, in exchange, for money, drugs, or favors.

This list is not exhaustive! God provided Moses with a "laundry list" of sexually immoral practices in Leviticus 18:1-24. Take time to read it for yourself.

By participating in one of these, you are breaking God's command and quite possibly breaking covenant with your spouse! Do not forget we are entering into a covenant. We are united to our spouse as one flesh and spirit. We defile the marriage bed when we introduce "someone else" into that covenant.

Let us then commit ourselves to live pure and godly lives, not solely for the sake of our marriages, but for the sake of our own body, soul and spirit and for the sake of our own relationship with God.

C. SEXUAL INTIMACY AND MARITAL DUTY

1. Sexual Intimacy

> Paul addresses sexual immorality in virtually every letter that he writes. In fact, because of the amount of sexual immorality bombarding the believers in Paul's day, he makes an eye-opening observation in 1 Corinthians 7:1-2(NIV):

> *"Now for the matters you wrote about: It is good for a man not to marry. But since there is so much immorality, each man should have his own wife, and each woman her own husband."*

> He elaborates on this in verses 8-9(NIV):

> *"Now to the unmarried and to the widows I say: It is good for them to stay unmarried, as I am. But if they*

cannot control themselves, they should marry, for it is better to marry than to burn with passion."

Because of man's lack of self-control, Paul encourages believers to marry. He reinforces this counsel in 1 Timothy 5:14 as he instructs young widows to remarry and have children. God designed men and women to be attracted to each other. As those relationships flourish, our level of intimacy grows. As intimacy grows, passion grows. Paul, is saying, rather than fall into sexual immorality, specifically fornication, we are to marry. We are to come into spiritual covenant with one another.

SPECIAL NOTE TO THE UNMARRIED: THE DEEPER THE LEVEL OF INTIMACY (HAND-HOLDING, HUGGING, KISSING, TOUCHING) THE DEEPER THE PASSION. IT IS OFTEN WHEN PASSION IS AT ITS HIGHEST, THAT PEOPLE ATTEMPT TO EXERCISE SELF-CONTROL, TO NO AVAIL. IF WE ARE GOING TO LIVE PURE LIVES, WE MUST EXERCISE SELF-CONTROL FROM THE ONSET. SET LIMITS BEFORE YOU EVEN BEGIN DATING. DON'T LET THE WORLD LIE TO YOU! IT IS POSSIBLE FOR A RELATIONSHIP TO FLOURISH, WHILE KEEPING THE LEVEL OF INTIMACY IN CHECK.

Let us be clear that sexual intimacy is to be reserved for marriage. I am a firm believer, as established in Scripture, that God intends marriage to be between one man and one woman. I also contend, based on 1 Corinthians 7:2, above, that sexual relations are reserved for one husband and one wife. A covenant couple! There are no gray areas for the unmarried, adulterers, homosexuals, or polygamists. The scripture says, "Each man should have his own wife, and each wife her own husband."

2. Marital Duty

"The husband should fulfill his marital duty to his wife, and likewise the wife to her husband. The wife's body does not belong to her alone but also to her husband. In the same way, the husband's body does not belong to him alone but also to his wife."

1 Corinthians 7:3-4(NIV)

The Bible is clear that we have a marital duty to meet the emotional and sexual needs of our spouse. The expression of sexual intimacy becomes then the 'selfless giving of ourselves' to meet the needs of our spouse. Sexual intimacy is not the relinquishing of ourselves to their demands. What does it mean to fulfill our marital duty?

To fulfill our marital duty means that we strive to meet our spouse's needs. It is well known that husbands and wives intimate needs are different. For the most part, husbands' needs are physical while wives' needs are more emotional and relational. This is not a "cookie cutter" observation, individuals may be different, but as a whole, is generally correct. Husbands must then learn how to meet their wives' needs for emotional and relational intimacy and wives must learn how to meet the physical needs of their husbands.

Look up 1 Corinthians 7:5 and copy it in the space provided below: _____

_____

_____

_____

SEX IS NOT A WEAPON!

SEX IS NOT A BARGAINING CHIP!

SEX IS NOT TO BE TAKEN BY FORCE!

There is liberty in marriage, but that liberty cannot jeopardize God's Word or your marriage covenant.

3. TWO THINGS THAT CAN JEOPARDIZE YOUR MARRIAGE COVENANT

Let us discuss two things that can threaten the sexual integrity of your marriage.

a. Introducing others into your relationship. When you utilize visual aids, pornography, and especially other people, you step over the line of liberty into sin.

b. Secondly, if your actions demean the other person and
are only pursued for your own personal gratification,
you have overstepped the line of liberty.

Are there times that you can earnestly deprive one
another?

Deuteronomy states that for purity's sake we should abstain
from sexual activity during the uncleanness of the wife's
monthly cycle. The only other time is by "mutual consent," for a
specified period of time, for the purpose of prayer. (See: 1
Corinthians 7:5)

According to Paul, that time should not be a lengthy
period and then you are to come together again so that
Satan will not tempt you because of your lack of self-
control.
God desires us to enjoy each other as husbands and
wives intimately. He desires godly offspring, but also
emotional, physical, and spiritual oneness. Strive then to
keep your marriage beds pure by keeping yourself pure
and by honoring your spouse's needs.

NOTES

_____

_____

_____

_____

_____

_____

_____

_____

_____

_____

_____

_____

_____

_____

_____

_____

_____

_____

7

Raising Godly Children

"Fix these words of mine in your hearts and minds; tie them as symbols on your hand and bind them on your foreheads. Teach them to your children, talking about them when you sit at home, and when you walk along the road, when you lie down and when you get up. Write them on the doorframes of your houses and on your gates, so that your days and the days of your children may be many in the land."

Deuteronomy 11:18-21(NIV)

Children are a precious gift from God that He "entrusts" to you to raise, nurture and train in godly fear and admonition. As parents, you are the individuals that will have the most impact on your child's faith. We cannot underestimate the power of parental influence.

A. THE POWER OF PARENTAL INFLUENCE

In the scripture above, God instructs parents to fix His words on their own hearts and then teach them to their children. It is clear from this passage that it is not the job of the preacher or the Sunday school teacher to train up your child. It is yours! Sunday school class should not be the first place they hear about godly ideas. It should be a place where the godly principals that they have learned at home are reinforced.

Scripture records the power of parental influence in the lives of some of Israel's most well known kings. Let us look at three together:

Jehoshaphat: Read 2 Chronicles 17:3 and then record how this man was influenced by the faith of his family. _____

_____

_____

_____

Uzziah: Read 2 Chronicles 26:4 and then record how this man was influenced by his father's faith. _____

_____

_____

_____

Ahaziah: Read 1 Kings 22:52 and then record how his father and mother influenced this man. _____

_____

_____

These scriptures demonstrate that parents have the ability to influence their children positively or negatively. Very simply, a child can be, and is, trained in the way they should go.

B. TRAINING A CHILD

"Train up a child in the way he should go, and when he is old he will not turn from it."

Proverbs 22:6(NIV)

Notice God tells us not to simply tell them the way they should go, but to train them up in the way they should go.

1. Fix the Word on Your Heart

   According to Deuteronomy 11, as parents, we are to fix the word of God in our minds and on our hearts. We must not only teach the valuable principles found in God's Word to our children, but we must live them out before them as well. You are a "role model" for your children! In many cases, you are the only role model. They desire to be like you and will mimic what you do! Children who watch their parents live lives submitted to the lordship of Jesus Christ are far more likely to do so also.

2. Not Just Idle Words

Take a moment to look up Deuteronomy 32:46-47 and record it below: _____

_____

_____

The Word of God is not just a book of good ideas. The Word of God is life! Taking that to heart means that you understand the need to give that "life" to your family everyday. Just as you would not withhold life-giving food from your family, you cannot afford to withhold God's life-giving Word either.

C. TRAINING UP A CHILD REQUIRES DISCIPLINE

This training, like any other training, is not an easy task. It requires discipline. No good training will be devoid of discipline. Raising godly children is no exception. Discipline, however, is a "hairy" subject in our society. To spank or not to spank! Should we use grounding, time-outs, or naughty chairs? Should we discipline at all?

The Bible is not silent on the subject of correction and discipline. Before we look at what scripture says…let us lay down some ground rules!

#1: To discipline in anger is to punish!

#2: To discipline in love is to correct.

This may not sound to important now, but as you read God's Word, you will see why knowing this is important.

1. Does God Believe in Discipline?

Jesus said in Revelation 3:19(NIV):

"Those whom I love I rebuke and discipline."

Let us look together at some other scriptures relating to discipline. Look up and record them below:

a. Hebrews 12:7-8: _____

_____

_____

b. Proverbs 22:15: _____

_____

_____

c. Proverbs 23:12-14: _____

_____

_____

These scriptures help reinforce the necessity of godly discipline.

2. Healthy Discipline Imparts Wisdom

How should we discipline?

With the necessity of discipline being established, let us turn our attention to the question of "How we should discipline?" I am not going to get into a debate on

"method." What I am going to do is point to one Scripture that may help you determine if the method you are
using is effective.

*"The rod of correction imparts wisdom, but a child left
to itself disgraces his mother."*

Proverbs 29:15

The goal of healthy discipline is to impart wisdom. Discipline that does not correct, but is purely to punish
wrongdoing does not impart wisdom. In fact, improper
discipline can actually harm a parent's relationship with
their child.

3. Embittering our Children

Take a moment look up and record the following passages:

Colossians 3:21: _____

_____

Ephesians 6:4:_____

_____

Exasperate means to anger, embitter or enrage. Discipline motivated by anger can cause a child to emotion-
ally separate himself or herself from that parent. It then
becomes very hard for that parent to train that child in
the ways of righteousness and holiness. It is good for
families to evaluate and discuss discipline in their

homes on a regular basis. There are four "musts" that should be incorporated into that process.

4. The Four "Musts":

a. Husbands and wives must be in agreement to the method (spanking, time-outs, groundings) that will be used. This is especially true for blended families and step-parents. (There should be no double standards when it comes to blended families. Each of you should determine the method and both have the authority to exercise it within your home.) This should be communicated often to each other and to the children!

b. We must be supportive of each other's decisions. (Do not let the child undermine your solidarity as parents.)

c. We must establish a form of discipline that "actually" and "effectively" corrects. Children respond differently to different methods of discipline. If time-outs do not work, do not rule out spanking. If spanking is ineffective, do not rule out grounding.

d. Lastly, we must never, never, never discipline in anger!

Pastor's Note

One area that we discuss with prospective couples is the aspect of planning. We encourage couples to not make any major life decisions for at least a year. This gives them time to discuss financial considerations, educational goals, and career goals. We also encourage couples to discuss "if" they want to have children. How many? When? And yes, even methods of prevention, emphasizing that abortion is never an option. For those unable to have children we encourage them to explore the possibility of adoption and foster parenting. These are important topics that should be discussed during this session. Make certain that each person knows and understands the other's real position on these issues.

NOTES

_____

_____

_____

_____

_____

_____

_____

_____

_____

8

Leaving and Cleaving

"For this reason a man will leave his father and mother and be united with his wife, and they will become one flesh."

Genesis 2:24(NIV)

Although there seems to be clear-cut roles in Scripture for parents in raising their children, the Bible is interestingly silent on their responsibilities once they are married. In many marriages there is no parental involvement ... including encouragement. On the other end of that spectrum ... mommy's telephone number is speed dial number one! Not having a proper perspective of parental involvement can devastate a young marriage from the very beginning. It can cause hard feelings, strained relationships, and a general sense of discord.

A. FROM COVERING TO COVERING

Genesis 2:24, above, tells us that for this reason a man will leave his father and mother. One reason that a child comes out from under his or her parent's covenant covering is to "cleave to his wife" or in other words to establish their own covenant covering.

We see an amazing thing happen on a couple's wedding day. Look up Genesis 2:22 and record it below:_____

_____

_____

_____

In this passage, the woman is brought by the Father to be presented to the husband. This is symbolic of her coming out from under his covering. Then in Genesis 2:24 the man leaves his father and mother's covering and cleaves to his wife. The two then become one flesh as they enter into their own covenant relationship with God!

We use rings, vows and ceremony to memorialize this new union.

It is here the role of the parent changes.

B. MARRIAGE MENTORS

As parents we are preparing our children for this. We are preparing to release them back into the hands of God.

The same God who is sovereign over our marriage is the same God who will be sovereign over theirs.

Parents, then, move from the role of provider and protector to the role of "mentor." They are to remain involved by infusing wisdom and encouragement when needed, but by also knowing when to let their children be free to make their own mistakes. It is this type of balance that will earn a person the honor and respect that the Bible, so rightly, says that parents deserve.

Unfortunately, for many, marriage is a means of abandoning the relationships they have with their parents. For many it is a way of escaping the abuse, ridicule and torment they experienced. However, God did not design the marriage covenant as an escape mechanism and unfortunately many of those people carry that same bad behavior into their own marriages.

C. HONORING FATHER AND MOTHER

"Honor your father and your mother, so that you may live long in the land the Lord your God is giving you."

Exodus 20:12(NIV)

1. God Places High Regard on Parenting

God has placed high regard on the position of a parent. Take a moment to look up and record the following passages of scripture:

Leviticus 19:3 _____

_____

_____

Exodus 21:15-17 _____

_____

_____

These are some pretty strong sentiments on the necessity of respecting our fathers and mothers. Disrespecting
your parents in the Old Testament meant death! I high-
light these scriptures to show you the significance
placed on honoring our parents.

2. Honoring Our Parents

Many of you may be saying, "My parents did not live
godly lives, in fact, they abused me, beat me and
insulted me. How can I honor that?" It is simple, but not
easy. We are called to honor the "godly role" that they
hold. We are to honor them, not because of their obedience as parents, but as a testimony of your faith and trust
in God.

Take a few moments to read 1 Samuel 26:1-25

In this chapter, we see that David honored King Saul,
although Saul repeatedly tried to kill David. Many
would have said, David would have been "just" in killing
Saul and maybe he would have been, but David said, "I

will not touch the Lord's anointed." God took care of David because David honored Saul's position as king. God will take care of you as you honor your father and mother's role as parents.

3. Other Ways to Honor Your Parents

Take a few moments, look up, and record the following passages:

Proverbs 13:1: _____

_____

_____

Proverbs 29:3: _____

_____

_____

Proverbs 23:22 _____

_____

_____

Proverbs 28:24: _____

_____

_____

1 Timothy 5:8:_____

_____

_____

In Matthew 15:3-8, Jesus rebuked the Pharisees and teachers of the law for using tradition to nullify God's command to honor father and mother. Some of you can easily "honor" because you were raised in good homes by godly parents. Others must "honor" simply out of your love and obedience for God. Honor the positions that they hold and remember this from Ephesians 6:2(NIV) ...

"Honor you father and mother, which is the first commandment with a promise, that it may go well with you and that you may enjoy long life on the earth."

Pastor's Note

It is important to emphasize to each prospective couple that once they are married they are no longer responsible for honoring one set of parents, but two. Each person must realize the importance of not simply recognizing their spouse's family as being related, but really receiving them as family.

Parents want to be included in your lives even if you have left their covering! Be fair with how you divide your time (especially around holidays), communicate often, and do not be afraid to include them in some of the things you do!

NOTES

_____

_____

_____

_____

_____

_____

_____

_____

_____

_____

_____

_____

_____

_____

_____

_____

_____

_____

9

Conclusion

Pastor's Note

The last session that we normally provide is a session that we have called: "Wholeness and Healing." This is a longer session by nature. It is a time of openness and sharing designed to address any past hurts, emotional "baggage," unconfessed sin, past abuse or neglect. It is a time of confession and prayer. It is imperative that both people enter the marriage covenant whole in spirit, soul, mind and body. In this way, both individuals can contribute to the health and vitality of their marriage covenant.

10

Dayspring Community Church

SAMPLE GUIDELINES FOR THE SACRED MARRIAGE COVENANT

We believe the institution of marriage was established by God and is a sacred covenant between one man and one woman. This covenant is not to be entered into lightly. As a minister of the gospel of Jesus Christ, I believe that I will stand before God for those I bring into this sacred union and so I carry a deep conviction regarding the proper preparation for this ceremony. I am not interested in merely performing legal weddings. I am responsible for preparing couples for a life-long covenant between them and our precious Heavenly Father.

There are four required elements that I have included that I believe will help properly prepare both partners for a healthy, Christ-centered marriage.

1. The prospective husband and wife must both be Born-Again. (Born-Again being defined as having accepted Jesus Christ as Lord and Savior of their lives.)

   a. In Scripture, I could only find two weddings mentioned at which God was the officiate. The first is in the book of Genesis 2:22-25.

   "Then the Lord God made a woman from the rib he had taken out of the man, and he brought her to the man. The man said, "This is now bone of my bone and flesh of my flesh; she shall be called 'woman' for she was taken out of man." For this reason, a man will leave his father and mother and be united to his wife, and they will become one flesh. The man and his wife were both naked, and they felt no shame."

   In the above scripture, God brought two sinless people together as husband and wife, for the scripture states "they were both naked, and they felt no shame."

   The second example is a spiritual reference regarding the Marriage Supper of the Lamb. The Marriage Supper of the Lamb (Rev. 19:9) is the uniting of the bridegroom, Jesus Christ, who is without sin, to the bride of Christ.

   The Bride of Christ is a reference to the church, the body of Christ. This Church is described in Ephesians

5:27 as being "without stain or wrinkle or any other blemish, but holy and blameless."

Therefore, a man and woman who are both born-again meet the precedent set in Scripture. As believers in Jesus Christ, they are both new creations in Christ Jesus. The old has passed, the new has come. They are declared to be the righteousness of God in Christ, because of the sacrifice of His Son.

b. It is also my contention that this union only be established between two believers because the purpose of the ceremony is to establish a covenant. Ephesians 5:22-30 and Colossians 3:18-19 give specific guidance to the nature and roles of husbands and wives. In each, there are specific references made such as "Submit as to the Lord" and "Love as Christ loved the Church." It would not be conceivable for couples to live up to these expectations unless they each have a relationship with our Lord and Savior Jesus Christ. It is when we understand our covenant relationship with Jesus Christ that our marriage covenant with our spouses can flourish and grow.

2. One year of fruit recognition.

"By their fruit you will recognize them. Do people pick grapes from thorn bushes, or figs from thistles? Like-

wise, every good tree bears good fruit, but a bad tree bears bad fruit. A good tree cannot bear bad fruit, and a bad tree cannot bear good fruit."

Matthew 7:16-18

It is not always immediately evident whether a tree is good or bad. Seasons must come and go and fruit borne before a clear picture is visible regarding the nature of that tree. The same is true with people. It is not always possible to glean a clear picture of a person's life from the perspective of just a few short weeks or months. Evidence of a changed life and a person's commitment to living for Christ, most often, must be evidenced over a longer season of time. Therefore it is my policy, not to consider bringing a couple into such a sacred covenant without clear evidence that they are *both* committed to living, loving and serving Jesus Christ. In most cases, a year is sufficient to gauge *each individual's* commitment and steadfastness.

If it becomes evident that one or both of the individuals is not committed to the Christ-centered life, then I could not in good conscious perform that ceremony. Marriage is a sacred covenant and not a contract! It must be honored and protected.

3. Marital Counseling

a. During this year of recognition, the prospective couple would be required to attend 10 months of marital counseling designed to strengthen the couple's commitment to one another and to uncover and address any potential problems that could jeopardize the success of their marriage.

b. Each month the couple would attend one- 45-minute session addressing one of ten topics. Below is a list of the topics required to be covered:

1. What is a Covenant relationship?

2. The role of the Husband

3. The role of the Wife

4. Children (Child rearing, discipline, step-kids, and planning)

5. Finances: Overview of Scriptural Finances

6. Finances: Practical: Setting up of a budget and debt management

7. Sex: (Male/Female perspectives, It's beauty within the bonds of marriage.)

8. Communication: (Key to a healthy marriage)

9. Honoring Fathers and Mothers (Relationships with In-Laws)

10. Wholeness/Healing: This is a longer session by nature. It is a time of openness and sharing in order to discuss past hurts, emotional baggage, unrepented sin, past abuse and/or neglect. It is a time of prayer and confession. It is imperative that both people enter the marriage with a sense of wholeness.

4. An Appraisal Interview

At the completion of the counseling sessions, the couple will join my wife and I for an informal appraisal session. During this session we will discuss any area, which may need attention and give the couple a chance to reflect upon what they have learned. It is here that, the couple, not I, will decide if they feel prepared to continue on to the ceremony. At this point in the process, any reservations I might have would have been addressed during the counseling sessions.

If, upon review of these guidelines, you would like to pursue this sacred covenant then please contact Pastor Scott Burr at xxx-xxx-xxxx to set up an initial interview.

CPSIA information can be obtained
at www.ICGtesting.com
Printed in the USA
JSHW031239140521
14709JS00001B/36